◼ Curios

Publication of this book was supported by grants from the National Endowment for the Arts and the Greenwall Fund of The Academy of American Poets

Curios

Judith POEMS
Taylor

Sarabande  Books

LOUISVILLE, KENTUCKY

Managing Editor
Sarabande Books, Inc.
2234 Dundee Road, Suite 200
Louisville, KY 40205

LIBRARY OF CONGRESS CATALOGING-IN-PUBLICATION DATA

Taylor, Judith, —
Curios : poems / by Judith Taylor.
p.   cm.
ISBN 1-889330-44-2 (cloth: alk. paper). —
ISBN 1-889330-45-0 (pbk. : alk. paper)
I. Title.
PS3570.A94156C87   2000
811'.54—dc21   99-31945
CIP

Cover painting: *Allegory of Touch*, by Richard Piccolo.
Provided courtesy of the artist.

Cover and text design by Charles Casey Martin.

Manufactured in the United States of America.
This book is printed on acid-free paper.

Sarabande Books is a nonprofit literary organization.

For my sister, Joan Nissman

Acknowledgments

Grateful acknowledgment to the editors of the following publications in which these poems first appeared, sometimes in different versions:

The American Poetry Review: "Around the Corner," "Excess," "Only You Can Prevent Forest Fires," "Wardrobe of Air"

The American Voice: "Chekhovian Dream Hum," "Unnatural Fuchsia"

The Antioch Review: "Instructions to Her Next Husband"

Arshile: "Day-Glo"

Boston Review: "In the Country"

Green Mountains Review: "Pastorale," "Unclothed"

Luna: "Paper Dolls," "Reality," "The Underbelly of Days"

The Marlboro Review: "Eye Shadows," "Scary Movies"

Quarterly West: "In Private," "Religious Instruction"

The Salt Hill Journal: "Of Unknown Etiology"

Sheila-Na-Gig: "Assorted Holiday Favors"

The Spoon River Poetry Review: "Legacy," "Lovers," "Mask, "Other Than Odalisque," "Page From a Pillow Book," "Rice Paper," "Without Anesthesia" (originally published as "Emma in Cornwall")

Third Coast: "Imagination"

Two Rivers Review: "Domestic"

"Eye Shadows" is reprinted in *The Pushcart Prize XXIII: The Best of the Small Presses*, 1999 (Wainscott, NY: Pushcart Press, 1999).

I would like to thank the Vermont Studio Center and the MacDowell Colony for their generous support.

While writing this book I was cheered on and inspired by many friends. My especially deep gratitude to Ann Beckerman, Molly Bendall, Elena Karina Byrne, Patricia Cohan, Cathy Colman, Fred Dewey, Candace Falk, Lise Goett, Brenda Hillman, Janet Kaplan, Peter Marcus, and David Robbins. To Sharon Bryan and Stefanie Marlis, who opened the gate, *domo arigato*.

Bouquets to Sarah Gorham, Jeffrey Skinner, and the Sarabande staff.

Table of Contents

The most difficult performance in the world is acting naturally, isn't it?

—Angela Carter

Unnatural Fuchsia

I try to outdo reality, which tends to dress modestly.
Saw myself stroking a harp wearing a snood.
So why not take up the art of the tambourine or zither?
The siren call of a fictional life.
Practice separating your vowels from your consonants.
There are certain sentences I will never say aloud.
What's that roiling on the table, bouncing off the wall?
Mood, mood.
I got tired of pulling away from the prevailing winds.
Now I let them buoy me, bless me a little, before they knock me about.

Reality

Three horses standing in a field, heads down, still.
For a small moment I had two sisters.
A mother came home from the hospital without a baby.
They told me to forget all about it, and I did.
My living sister found the letters of condolence in our mother's closet.
Puzzled, she brought them to me.
I still don't understand about the secret underskin of families.
From the car the horses were not alive, but made of velvet.

Scary Movies

My nurse Kitty plays a funny game.
Is Kitty in the closet? Kitty, are you behind the couch?
Christ of the Cross appears in my bedroom.
Since I'm a Jewish child, I'm surprised.
Kitty pounces on me from behind the drapes.
Skinny Jesus with holes in his skin, drops of button blood.
I'm going to get you!
I hide my head in Mother's lap at the movies during the newsreels.
We're dropping bombs on bad people.
It's only make-believe, darling, she says.

Paper Dolls

They taught us to cut them out in school, rows of identical girls, a pattern.
One breaks off from the rest, or an arm appears, a leg, from another doll.
Now she is excessive, interesting.
As a child I saw a film: a man stood over a beautiful laughing woman,
      raised his riding crop.
The scene ended and I wanted to know what happened to women like her.
Since then I've heard this tale many times, its varying degrees of clumsy
      violence.
Do the scissors make the mistake, or does the hand?

Religious Instruction

Mother bade me enter the rose-smelling closet where I assiduously
  studied the texts.
O Litany of Blue Robe, O Sacred Book of Shoes.
And the Mystery: why does taffeta change colors in every fold as if
  light were trapped there?
A child tracing curves of necklines: some scalloped, some deep and
  smooth as moons.
Stroking foamy chiffon, burrowing into fur.
We were votaries of the goddess of costume.
My heart pumped roadways to mother-love, to glove-love, to Saks
  Fifth Avenue.

Shuttered

—after Odilon Redon, *Yeux Clos*

A woman's head with closed eyes rises out of water.

The sky smudged dark at the horizon as if someone knew what I needed.

Is her head attached to a body under the sea's creamy glass?

Water's a kind of architecture you can step in and out of—but only
      sometimes.

Once in school I was instructed not to speak for a week.

We passed notes back and forth, my scrawl glowing mean as a brand.

The keyboard's missing some keys, the scissors snap on nothing.

Funny Hats

Mother placed a shiny black bug with purple spots and a tiny veil on me.
Insect hats don't go with Dignity.
There's an old photo I love: she's moored a darling truffle to the side of
  her head.
That must have been in the Before days, before she took the Vow of
  Sacred Cow.
Though the saleswoman smiled, her eyebrows gloomed.
I thought of myself as Alice or Dorothy, on loan to the middle class.
I wanted her to wear a large bird or a bathtub on her head, to *prove*
  she was my mother.

Mistakes

As he put me on the train to college, Father said, Don't make any mistakes.

I became the Princess of Mistakes.

The interesting thing about looking out a window—it tells the truth, but only one truth.

All vision is blandishment, I didn't know that then.

Someone was always saying, Don't Touch.

One of my more persistent mistakes: not knowing why I couldn't have everything I wanted.

Everything can be changed into everything, I heard another ten-year-old say.

Coast to Coast

Stop playing the piano for years, and you can't play arpeggios anymore.

Here, I'm no longer experienced in slush-walking.

Back then, everything was fattening *and* good for you.

Farrago is one of my favorite words. Also *incarnadine. Lollygag.*

    Shambolic. Reportage.

In Vermont there's a lot of emphasis on maple flavor, which I like.

Did you know a *passerine* is a bird that grips branches?

Do you know what *gazump* means?

One can eat chocolate peanut butter frozen yogurt every season in L.A.

The tintinnabulation of the Good Humor truck still rings in my good ear.

Baba Yaga

Baba Yaga's hut struts on stringy chicken legs.
And hey, that's Baba Y. navigating the night sky in her mortar and pestle!
Russian witch of my childhood—power for good, or outrageousness.
Lilac Fairy, Little Goose Girl: the nicer side of the mirror.
Haven't you noticed how my teeth grind when you ask me to be rational?
The Brothers Grimm believe women need the Prince.
I believe in plot, my dear, only when it suits me.

Excess

A baby's fingers, blossoming petals.
The holiday presence of her white crocheted sweater.
Your planet of longing spinning slower, wonky.
Neighbor children, I wish you'd shut up when I want to think!
How you never wanted to be pregnant, how fat you'd get.
You diet, take off excess flesh, put it back on.
Do the stars hiss when they slash across the sky, cooling down?
Get a grip on yourself, said Mother often.

Only You Can Prevent Forest Fires

To live overpowered, devoted to my brilliant mistakes.

Every woman needs one Mr. Wrong in her life.

For emergencies, a cocktail of Valium and white wine.

Teeter-tottering toward stiletto assignations.

Bed of spikes, bed of fur, bed of silk—is there any difference?

I look to find things to dislike about Mr. Wrong: the grease on his tie,
     the worn-down heels of his klutzy brown shoes.

When Anna Karenina stares down that train, I want to yell, Stop,
     honey, no man is worth it!

I believe this six out of every seven days.

What is fiction, but another kind of mirror?

Eye Shadows

All aristocratic men wore makeup at the court of Louis Quinze.

The seducer Lovelace looked foppish but was lethal.

Since then, men's cosmetics have taken a precipitous fall.

Now he's ill-tempered as she struggles with her mascara.

In the moonlight, no one wears makeup, and if there's blush left on her
      face, it's blanched out.

She sits on him, and he's her rocking horse, familiar, steady, silver.

A Visitation From One Sort of Angel

Cars honk more plaintively in New York than anywhere else.

A window, far down, opening by means of a red sleeve.

Things seem this way when you're eighteen floors up.

I want some minutes to be longer than others.

If I were telling a story about a real angel, he'd appear at the casement,
and knock, his silly wings beating.

Do my slow high-rise minutes ever add up to his driving-the-highway
minutes?

The doorman buzzes up, I open the extraordinary door.

When young, I misread Rilke's angels as sexual presences.

Now I know the poor beautiful body in real time is what I've always
craved.

The Demon Lover

This won't be at all like Hamlet.

I will not be the kind of ghost you are used to.

I will do invisible naughty things to you while you are teaching, while
     you are dining, while you are singing.

Your chalk will suddenly screech on the blackboard.

You will drop your fork into the red center of your Porterhouse.

You will cover your privates with the score of a cantata or motel—
     oops!—motet.

Swooping and bungeeing around you for the rest of your days, I'm
     making mischief: a woman playful, not wholly unkind, logistical.

Sky Writing

I remember the days when pure world used to swim underwater.
Please, let's not talk about anything serious, my eyes ache.
The sun booms over us, shadows pointing long opinionated fingers.
Is that a cigarette burn smoldering in the sky?
Money, money, money—you'd think we lived in a Balzac novel.
Both of us, or neither, capable of betrayal.
Let's wait for *l'heure bleue* when shadows slip back into their objects,
    when mothy illusions console us.

Domestic

When a relationship goes blah, heaven goes on purpling itself quite
      nicely without our Oohs, our Aahs.
See, I noticed one day that his hands were a kind of lobstery pink.
The mind's seduced by the idea of knots and another's shallow breathing.
The teakettle squats, waiting to be filled, at the very least to the middle.
Oscar Wilde said: "Being natural is simply a pose."
He could have noticed the new smile I purchased for full price.

Instructions to Her Next Husband

What shall I put in my experimental trousseau?
A paint box, a pint of scotch, a box of chocolates.
A set of masks with pleasant expressions.
Instructions on how to bow and curtsey, dance the reel.
I don't want any smoldering hotcakes for breakfast.
No indigo looks either, take some pills instead.
If you see me staring out the window, tiptoe past wearing a bear's head.

In Private

Dawn, I feel my face scuff the pillow, but I'm asleep.

My fanatic ghosts appear, doll-size.

They allow me to dress and undress them.

Half-understood gestures are my destiny.

Everyone has crimes to hide from.

The figures smile ambiguously, whisper sedition.

Lacy pleasures, what do you have in common with shadows?

I can't stop computing the long division of my sadness.

Costly

The future sprints in front of you, wears silver shorts and running shoes.
She is gorgeous and fleet, you cannot envy her.
You drink champagne, and when the cork hits the ceiling, your heart
pounds.
You finger silk before you wear it, you touch the pear before you eat it.
Pear with a red glow, pear with a holiday body.
Your little flame of longing, like the eternal light in the temple that never
gets extinguished.

Chekhovian Dream Hum

I was Masha in *The Three Sisters* and didn't know my lines.

Act II, to cover up, drank pints of tea from the samovar.

I forced myself to go through the whole play.

Sometimes humming with my lover, Vershinin.

Moscow: how we yearn to go there, and never do.

My Russian-born Jewish grandmother fled from the Cossacks yet
identified with the aristocracy, who knows why?

When my sister Irina said, "To Moscow, to Moscow," I wept.

Masha: the most restless and shadowy of the highborn sisters.

Gliding across the stage dressed in my carmine yearning.

Told my dream at lunch where it bored everyone.

What a Chekhovian moment that was!

Imagination

Stop reading in the dark, it will ruin your eyes!

If you could enter a picture or book, slip into it, what would be required
of you *there*?

Your model Alice was at ease with the Red Queen.

And Dorothy chatted with the mechanical man Tik-Tok and Princess
Langwidere, who changed her head whenever she felt like it.

The woman in Lessing's novel walked through a wall into another world.

After a while, *there* becomes domestic.

Today a head with crooked smile, tomorrow one with vanilla placidness.

A self wardrobe.

You're only crazy at the point you stop feeding the children.

Acting Wilde

Buttressed in bustle, gloves, and hat; beautifully martyred in a tight corset.

Snaps a fan open, shut, expressing her character's confidence, her
embroidered desires.

"I never travel without my diary. One should always have something
sensational to read in the train."

Her other role: faculty wife.

She's stopped smoking Viceroys, begun to drink.

She'd never realized before: she's shy!

Now she inhabits a creature who hasn't one wisp of doubt.

A contact lens burns—she twirls around, pops it out, says her next line
one-eyed.

Other Than Odalisque

I dream I'm the Belle of Alabama.

My harlequin glasses look out of place with my wasp waist.

Hiyall!

I have two costume changes: Pre-War yellow, Post-War green.

Some soldier is trying to get me out of my bodice.

I rap him on his Confederacy with my silk fan.

To win my respect, he rushes away to join the Bengal Lancers.

My waist a mere seventeen inches.

Southern women are skittish, unlike those unclothed gals hanging in
      Father's study.

Between Utterances

—after Edouard Vuillard, *Figure Seated by a Curtained Window*

If there were curtains like this in my world, I wouldn't need to leave it.
The woman's there for balance, shape, maybe she's sewing.
Vuillard's room: calm, silent, green.
Not to be able to touch any of it yet be glad.
Behind the curtains, the closed window, a stilled mouth.
I can leave a space simmering with talk any time I want to.
What I do on the other side is entirely my own business.

Achromatopia

She lived with a painter, lived with his eyes (known as an "eye").

Every vista seemed as though he'd envisioned it first.

The birches clustered—proud, archaic—crocuses spiking up around the
  slender trunks.

Everything tinted in Viridian, or a Venetian Red eeriness.

Once, she insisted she saw mere blue, plain yellow: a bad day.

Was looking at the world his way narrowing, or did it widen her own
  prison?

If only he'd recognized her authority, she would have used it more often.

Pastorale

Wine was being passed around and consumed.

In formation, swallows careened in the evening sky.

We wondered if this was a rehearsal for the long performance south.

Sometimes when I'm out in nature, it's so perfect.

Is this Hartley, or Hockney, or Hokusai?

I speculated aloud how many centuries we would have to go back to be
uncontaminated by art.

I secretly hoped for rain, an interesting, stuttering rain, good for thinking
about art.

"You want to see two daddy-longlegs mating? Or would you prefer to
see them dead?"

In the Country

The weather's acting like an adolescent: radical unhappiness, then blind
    joy.
Distance in the distance.
On nature walks, information about bugs and birds ballooned and
    hovered in a spot above the counselor's head.
Cartoon talk in a language I wouldn't learn.
That is why today I screamed when I saw a spider on my blanket.
Forests look inviting, but I like them to remain mysterious.
I like them to look like illustrations to *The Blue Fairy Book*, all Art
    Nouveau curlicue and flourish.
The ideal way I savor a forest is to say it, read it.

Bats

Last night I dreamed I was Japanese.

My fan intricate, disturbing.

Bats dove up and down the pale sky.

Why are most Japanese ghosts women?

My counterparts whispering from another millennium.

Ghosts: shy women.

I'm afraid of bats when awake.

I want something more than to hide myself, something less than revelation.

Page From a Pillow Book

All tulips are lovely, but I have a favorite.

Pillow Book: flotsam of days, kept in a wooden pillow.

I was with a married man: this was a dream.

I lied to his wife, yes, I would stop.

I looked out my window and saw them arguing.

Long ago I trained myself to sleep with someone's body tight around me.

The most beautiful tulips are the dark purple ones, love-bites.

Lovers

—after a screen portraying a scene from *The Tale of Genji*

Thank you for noticing the colors I'm wearing today.

You and I, we're on the suspension bridge between then and next,
    swaying a little.

See, the lovers drift in a pleasure boat where the water takes them, into
    sea-gold, sky-gold.

Her face lists down shyly, yet of the two, she writes better poems.

Literary History, no friend to women, says this of the Heian Era, so don't
    contradict me.

The picture isn't clear whether the lovers will be spared the usual fate.

You ask: What if one of the two knows how to swim and the other
    doesn't?

Oh, that's a question of an entirely different order, don't you think?

Weight of Hair

I feel like telling you a story.

Long ago, layered robes rain-rustled as they made love in their clothes.

Silk like green pines on the man-made island, like blue waves on the
    artificial lake.

Years of the dark room, and the screens opening up then closing on his
    smile.

He never realized that she wasn't like the swaying kelp where the seaward
    gatherer can come as often as he wants.

Do you think I don't leaven *my* images behind a pleated fan?

Her curtain of flowing hair, which masked her, swept the dust.

Mask

Woe to the unfortunate man who falls in love with her.
Japanese ghosts glide along the earth, having no feet.
Pines, the moon, seen through the ghost's lucent body.
Angry ghost, sad ghost, having once been abandoned by a lover.
She roams the glades, searching for him, always successful.
Shining as she never did when alive.
If his fate is just, then the ghost-woman becomes the hero.
He said: When you put on your mask, we had our purest sexual moment.

Rice Paper

After China, Japan seemed materialistic.

Outside restaurants, we studied the models of food.

A detective goes from dark place to dark place, seeking answers.

The pilgrimage to Hiroshima.

In silent gardens, the sun unmoving.

Down an alley, a gray cat, slow, with one eye.

Japan's euphonic taste—unrelenting as heat and as transforming.

The Buddha? A cool shadow to stand in.

There can be a light answer to a dark question, can't there?

Legacy

Mother's Japanese screen, its panorama of stopped time.

It was understood the screen would become mine when the day I did
    not want to come, came.

Afterward, I saw everything from the wrong end: faraway, hard to
    make out.

All life seemed exquisite, sad—here and disappearing, at the same instant.

When I sold her apartment, I agreed to toss the screen into the bargain.

I walked out to Michigan Avenue's clear sapphire darkness.

That night I *could* see, and the moon was an orange curved blade, the
    two sharp points cleaving toward each other.

Around the Corner

The day broods to its end in a bluish, useless way.

I'm sick of indoors, outdoors.

Isn't there a third place I could be?

I've a Japanese fan on which a geisha looks in a mirror.

You can tell a geisha by her hairdo and her sidelong look.

What would a geisha do on a day like this?

Dress her little girl attendants in kimonos that matched her own, take
  the whole retinue on a dance-walk two blocks to the teahouse to
  meet a "friend."

This could take . . . oh, maybe an hour?

The atmosphere's portentous, but I'm looking for tempo.

We Maenads

We maenads got drunk and wanted to party.
We never liked that guy Orpheus, he sang better than any of us.
On top of that, he wouldn't sleep with our beauties.
Boy, he came apart easily.

The Language of Yes

The money of the millennium's talking, crooning buy, buy, buy.
Will tomorrow bring a boa of Blue Chips, a ripped T-shirt of Futures?
It's Peoria in this molecularly dirty city.
My lips neoned in Spice over Tramp, toes licked red in Dangerous.
I wave one fishnetted footsie at you from across the notional room.
Why don't you walk over here, to the nomenclature of sex?
Console me, baby, with the beauty and froufrou of your refracted self.

The Language of No

Leaves molder (or is it molt?) at the foot of trees.

Your book on long-lost love has been published to terrible reviews.

The leopard bustier no longer fits you.

When you come to mind, people's thoughts turn glacier-blue, you're sure
of it.

An old firework flares up: lots of color, a big bang, then Poof! where is he?

Tomatoes taste like potatoes and potatoes taste like minnows.

That bobcat's on patrol, the one you'd tried to tame, calling out, "Here,
Tosca, here, Tosca."

The Language of Maybe

It's time: bring out the stopwatch of hesitation.

The world's being built all over again, this time by ants.

The oddest part of life is the heart's exhausted diminishment.

I lost the turquoise ring you gave me, I think in the Everglades, I think
    on purpose.

Maybe I'm sorry.

Why hide in a black dress if a bull chases you?

On a day like this, I crave a diet of burgundy and almonds to prove I
    exist.

In the artificial light of lamp and candle, everything's bathed in an aura
    of limited caring, measured anxiety.

Without Anesthesia

The time I climbed the Cornwall cliffs I imagined dying unheroically.

I hate that Emma Bovary drank rat poison.

It took a long time for her to die, while Charles blubbered at bedside.

If Emma lived in Cornwall, she'd end up clinging to a rock.

I used to identify with her type, not anymore.

If you're able to get down a cliff over a turbulent sea, a certain
     excitability drops away.

Of course, sensation lingers—it always does, ghost of the amputated part.

Home

One way to avoid scandals: wear sunglasses.

"Whoa, is that *your* jasmine?" "That's my jasmine."

The bobcat swaggered down my path like a model on a runway.

Then there was the night it took longer than it should to crush the
   tarantula.

I used a cowboy boot—pink suede.

Another way of avoiding scandals: don't go out.

Sometimes when we made love, I thought the room dissolved.

The pool cleaner snakes around the bottom, then lies still for hours.

After Image

The room, when photographed, reveals no color.
She opens the dictionary to the word *Norwegian*.
And considers this oracular, as it's snowing outside.
Her face troubled in the mirror, puzzled by an echo.
In the previous scene did they call her a "social butterfly"?
The dreamwind tears at the tops of the palms, almost defeating them.
A social butterfly lives alone while the century itches.
Her room, white as an egg, silent as a blizzard.

The Underbelly of Days

Some mornings I stumble awake into the presence of deer.

Where I live, a lot of staring between species occurs.

What does a fawn see: unhappy woman in maroon robe with undereye
circles?

This morning I awoke with words swinging from dreams.

As he embraced his wife, she looked straight at me, saying, "Lily, Lily,
Lily."

In the dream that was my name.

I try to open it, but there's no perfect door to lost things.

Natural Woman

Snails spit glistening threads on my poor pansies, chewed to lace.

Let me not hear one more rattler when I walk up the canyon!

Darwinian nineteenth century crepuscular dread overcomes me when the
      sun goes down and some *thing* scuttles in the attic.

That's a bit of a lie, but I've succeeded in saying crepuscular.

You could say I've a yes/no relationship with nature.

Sunning themselves on the patio, geckos, of whom I'm fond, do
      insouciant push-ups.

I swoosh my broom around, a warning to centipedes oozing their way
      across the carpet.

This is the deal: we all stay where we belong, and no one gets hurt.

Antiquity

It rained all day and night two hundred years ago.

They intoned *le jardin, la lune* there.

But we inferred the past from our camellia's droop, its pink heaviness.

The busky oak could have grown old in the Dordogne or Provence.

Sipping gimlets on the patio, our gestures pulling in the view for guests.

"She came to trust him with her disintegration."

Our life together wasn't picturesque.

Finally we agree: Los Angeles cannot masquerade as France.

On Lincoln Boulevard, pink-painted storefronts bellow: "Health-O-
    Rama," "Mattresses Reduced," "U-Haul."

Los Angeles Quotidian

The psychic brings out her tarot pack and reads me my fate.
Forget selling the house, wait till interest rates drop—May 8th, 2028.
Last night that almost commonplace jolt: once, fiercely, then no more.
The psychic says not to worry: when the Big One hits, I'll be in Rangoon,
      Hong Kong, Tierra del Fuego, Kuala Lumpur, Jakarta, lah-de-dah.
Certainly, the psychic's voice has a sibilance of authority.
Oh my god, the computer's making a horrible noise—or *is* it God?

Wardrobe of Air

The aroma-tissue-organic-orgasmic therapist liked my outfit.

Because it was yellow? Because it wasn't black?

It's hard to forge an identity when you and your baby sister are forced
to wear matching pinafores.

Lusting after the same man, a friend and I bought identical red suede
pumps.

The woman with the sailing cap and dead moonstone eyes wore gloves
to hide her hands.

"Men love it when I wear gloves."

If you know what a pinafore is, raise your hand.

After ten years, Mother's ghost clothes in my closet smell of dogwood.

Each time I travel, I choose clothes cautiously, as if embarking on a
honeymoon.

Nostradamus L.A. Style

Atlantis, that island paradise—good climate, lifestyle—sank.

The predicted disaster for L.A. this year is flood.

We could disappear at any moment, falling into the arms of Ancient
    History.

Someone might even believe we never existed.

My friend lay on the restaurant's floor, a maelstrom of paramedics in
    attendance.

I thought he was dead, but he wasn't.

After the big earthquake, I gathered up the shards and put them in a
    Westward Ho Food Bag.

Kramer: "Will some of us be able to breathe underwater in the year
    2000?"

Jerry: "Some of us."

Assorted Holiday Flavors

Her lover's at the rented (a) cottage, (b) cabin, (c) beach house, (d) condo.

Calls her from a pay phone while out buying butter for his family's
   baked potatoes.

Reports hitting some balls, shooting some rapids, shooting some views.

Her garden's wilting in the summer's slow arching hours.

Magnificents, Enchantments, Gloriannas loll open, embarrassing her
   with their lush to-be-plucked readiness.

She imagines him trembling at the edge of a declivity.

Tap, tap, tap goes the hummingbird on her window, as if to (a) warn her,
   (b) make her laugh.

Day-Glo

Wearing nothing but one silver watch between us.

Exiled to another boondock of desire, the Newark Hilton.

We could see two different skylines when we looked out the window.

The sun slatted across the bed, irradiating our whiteness.

The watch glittered but I turned my head from it.

Overpowered by and still devoted to illusion.

I can smell his skin, rogue's skin, warming up.

Of Unknown Etiology

I swallowed the wind that night but it had no weight.

An ordinary evening, masked and forthright.

I moved through labyrinthine hotel corridors that kept turning into
corners.

The letters of my name splintered, then reformed into other eradicable
designs.

Marriage can do this for you, and adultery has the same effect.

The moon slid across the sky, Roman coin, amulet.

Though I wore a green silk dress, I don't think he ever found me.

Cage of Crickets

A moon of bone glowing at the foot of the bed.

A blouse, missing a button, twisted on the floor.

Always a story behind the haze of curtains.

Like Oriental pearls, brought into being in the dark—those lovers for
     whom kisses will forever be passionate.

The clock sings its tractable minutes for them.

You can be sure that when one leaves, the other shudders, with sorrow
     and relief.

Remedy for Backache

While traveling in a plane coming back from seeing a married lover,
   place a tennis ball under your left buttock.
Remember your chiropractor says you're uneven, one hip hiked up, one
   pulled down.
Remember to press down on the tennis ball.
Don't remember it was he who gave it to you.
When the plane experiences turbulence, smile, what else is there to do?
Don't remember what happiness felt like.
Press down, even if it hurts.

Growl

Right now, you can't dial my laughter, that exhausted number.

Thank you very much, but that's a sorry apple of argument you're
handing me.

What does it matter if I say privacy and you say secrecy?

From my window it looks as if the grass is divided evenly between sun
and shadow.

You snap at the same postulates, like those boys who used to grab my
bra elastic, pull, and let go.

Your righteousness: pointed, narrow, with big Armani shoulders.

I won't stay grave much longer about "our issue," as I'm getting hungry
for pastrami on rye.

Jewel

Their sex last night a little scary.

The Goldberg Variations, over and over, on the boom box.

Tinny, attenuated, as if squeezed from a cheap metallic toy.

Gould's fingers, it seemed, had to press down hard to know what key
    they played in.

Above her wrist a bruise that doesn't hurt when she touches it.

Each of them tried to efface the other's elusiveness.

The bruise a radiance and she raises her arm to her mouth, licks it.

The Vast Green Sea

We are good friends now, more than anything else.
Which means we are more like the married than when we were first
      together, all the more adulterous.
Protean steam rises from tea: I see our future, comfortable though odd.
The wet soft grass shifting in the rain.
A gray bird I've never seen before flies past the window, its wings tipped
      with white brilliant as a painted eye!
It sits on an evergreen branch, flies to a maple, and oh, it surprises me
      just as I thought the world's calmed down so.
I wish you here, right now.
Totally unmemorized.

Unclothed

Parched by absences, we traveled to reach water, his coast, my coast.

The necklace of his breath, the belt of his sweat: acquisitions to stave
off loss.

Purchased at the price of loss.

Why did such bright hard light keep crowding the room?

I pretended angels were interested in us.

When I opened my eyes, I knew how the self swallows dissonance, which
leads to a kind of blankness.

I don't know if I've followed my heart's true requests.

Which heart?   Which one?   When?

Moorish Weather

At Haworth I saw a dress, small as a child's, that Charlotte Brontë wore.
Her front door opened to the cemetery, back door to the moor.
I've a photo of myself walking there, wind-whipped hair, holding a
    snippet of heather.
Bookish children hang suspended between fiction's phantasmagoria and
    an equally illusory future.
Grown up, we're found a few feet off the ground, hummingbird pilots of
    bemused purview.
The canny child preserves only her best illustrations, their permanent
    zealous colors.

She's Got Mail

I wanted everything connected to everything in a logical universe.
Tried humming the future before it splintered the glass.
Maybe the secret's simple: let the mirror reflect whatever's there.
Pacific curls slick the beach, crows echo above.
Mornings, each object on my bureau reminds me of itself, and so
    reappears.
Dawn remains silvery and purposefully enigmatic.
In time, the world begins to shape your stubborn mind.

Notes

The epigraph is from Angela Carter's story, "Flesh and the Mirror," in *Burning Your Boats: The Collected Short Stories.*

"Domestic"—The quotation in the penultimate line comes from Wilde's novel, *The Picture of Dorian Gray:* "Being natural is simply a pose, and the most irritating pose I know."

"Imagination"—Tik-Tok and Princess Langwidere appear in L. Frank Baum's *Ozma of Oz;* Tik-Tok in subsequent Oz books, as well. The Doris Lessing novel is *The Memoirs of a Survivor.*

"Acting Wilde"—Line three is from Wilde's *The Importance of Being Earnest.*

"In the Country"—*The Blue Fairy Book* is one of the collections of fairy tales (named for different colors) compiled by Andrew Lang in the late nineteenth century.

"Lovers"—Ono No Komachi and Izumi Shikabu of Japan's Heian Era are the writers referred to in this poem.

"Weight of Hair"—Line five is based on Kenneth Rexroth's version of an Ono No Komachi poem, found in his *Love Poems from the Japanese.*

"Natural Woman" is dedicated to Lin Nelson Benedek.

"Nostradamus L.A. Style"—Nostradamus, the sixteenth-century French astrologer and physician, wrote *Centuries*, a book of prophecies. The last two lines are dialogue from the television series *Seinfeld*.

The Author

Judith Taylor received her Ph.D. in
English from the University of California,
Berkeley. After teaching in the Writers'
Program at UCLA for fifteen years, she
now teaches poetry and literature in Los
Angeles. Her poems have appeared in
such journals as *The American Poetry
Review, Poetry, The Antioch Review,
Nimrod, Boston Review, Witness,* and
The American Voice. Among her honors

Tom Benedek

are the Portlandia Chapbook Contest for *Burning* (1999, The
Portlandia Group), the Aldrich Museum Emerging Poets Reading, the
Open Voice Poetry Award from the Writer's Voice of the West Side Y,
and a Pushcart Prize.